APPLES

A Cookbook

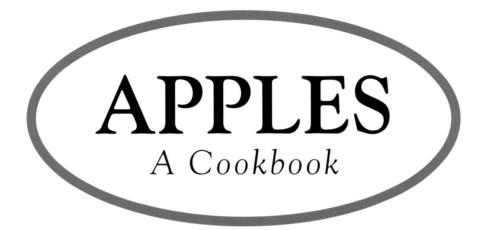

APPLES
A Cookbook

GREENWICH EDITIONS

A QUANTUM BOOK

This edition published by
Greenwich Editions
10 Blenheim Court
Brewery Road
London N7 9NT

ISBN 0-86288-145-5

QUMABK

This book was produced by
Quantum Books Ltd
6 Blundell Street
London N7 9BH

Printed in Singapore by Star Standard Industries Pte Ltd

ACKNOWLEDGMENTS

Our special thanks to those companies who generously
loaned us their beautiful wares: Country Floors,
Dean & DeLuca, Fitz and Floyd, Platypus, Jeffrey Weiss
New York, and especially Douglas Weiss at Pottery Barn
and Pauline Kelly at Zona.

INTRODUCTION
8

ONE
BREAKFAST
AND BRUNCH

Oat Griddle Cakes with Jonathan
Apples and Pecans
18

Rome Apple, Orange and
Prune Compote
20

Northern Spy Apple Fritters
22

Banana Muffins with
Dried Apples and Apricots
24

Apple-Hazelnut Muffins
24

Mcintosh Apple and
Sausage Pie
26

Winesap Apple Turnovers
28

Spiced Macoun Apple Bread
with Walnuts
30

TWO
SOUPS, SALADS
AND STARTERS

Northern Spy Apple
and Butternut Squash Soup
34

Mcintosh Apple and
Blue Cheese Bisque
36

Granny Smith
Apple-Onion Soup
with Celeriac
38

Radicchio, Chicory and
Golden Delicious Apple Salad
40

Wilted Greens with
Red Delicious Apples and Bacon
42

Cracked Wheat Salad with
Jonathan Apples and Mint
44

Smoked Turkey and
Gravenstein Apple Salad
46

Rome Apple and
Goat's Cheese Tartlets
48

Greening Apple
and Spinach Pate
50

THREE
MAIN COURSES

Baked Cortland Apples
with Sweet Potato Filling
54

Grilled Swordfish with
Lady Apple Butter
56

Trout Baked in
Parchment with
Northern Spy Apples
58

Barbecued Prawns with
Jonathan Apple and Quince Chutney
60

Red Snapper with
Empire Apples and Walnuts
62

Turkey Pie with
Newtown Pippins and Onions
64

Duck Breasts with Crab Apples
66

Chicken and Cortland Apple Couscous
68

Pork Chops with Rome Apple
and Rosemary Stuffing
70

Spareribs with
Apple Sauce Glaze
72

Grilled Veal Chops
and Granny Smith Apples
74

FOUR
ACCOMPANIMENTS

Braised Red Cabbage with
Northern Spy Apples
78

Caramelized Greening Apples
and Button Onions
78

Fresh Golden Delicious
Apple-Walnut Relish
80

Gingered Crab Apple Sauce
80

Carrot, Parsnip and
Granny Smith Apple Coleslaw
82

Three-Apple Butter
84

FIVE
DESSERTS

Cran-Apple Pie
88

Calvados Soufflé
90

Jonathan Apples Poached
in Red Wine
92

McIntosh Apple Crumble
with Vanilla Ice Cream
94

Winesap Apple Pudding
96

Candied Lady Apples
98

Granny Smith Apple Sorbet
100

Golden Delicious Apple
and Cinnamon Ice Cream
102

Macoun Apple Pie
104

Golden Delicious Apples with
Caramel and Biscuits
106

Baked Rome Apples
with Cointreau
108

Jonathan Apple Dumplings
110

Empire Apple and Pear Tarts
112

Hot Buttered Apple Juice
118

Calvados Punch
118

Calvados Spritzer
120

Apple Juice Spritzer
120

RECIPE LIST
122

RECIPE LIST BY APPLE
OR APPLE PRODUCT
124

SIX
BEVERAGES

Apple-Apricot Smoothie
116

Apple-Cranberry Iced Tea
116

INTRODUCTION

Versatile, enduring, delicate – these qualities describe the apple as a concept as well as a food. The apple is as much a part of the iconography of cooking and folk culture as a stove, a pot or a ladle; so much so that the mere mention of, say, apple pie is often enough to evoke images and memories that are inextricably associated with the pie: a picnic, a birthday, a family holiday gathering.

The apple is a common ingredient throughout most of the world's cooking. It can be manipulated in many ways, maintain its identity and still yield itself to its intended use. It can be sautéed, baked, fried, grilled or just sliced. It works wonderfully with meats, in salads, in desserts or by itself. An apple is a fruit that has a thin but tough skin, a very tough core, inedible seeds, and firm, fibrous meat that accounts for about 90 percent of its composition. Depending on the variety, apples can be sweet, juicy, tart, sour, even salty. As a cooking ingredient the apple usually does what you tell it to do. However, there are a few basic principles to keep in mind. The skin is a valuable ingredient, containing what many consider to be the essence of the apple's flavour, but it is useful in some recipes and obtrusive in others. The skin of an apple has a high concentration of fructose (natural fruit sugar) and a substance called pectin, which provides a gelatinous, thickening element to recipes such as jams or preserves. (Pectin can be extracted from apple skins, and is sold commercially in powder form.) In a recipe for apple sauce or apple butter (such as Gingered Crab Apple Sauce) where the pectin and fructose contribute highly to the final outcome of the dish, the skin can be cooked along with the meat and core and seeds (which also contain smaller amounts of fructose and pectin) to great advantage. After they have given off all they can give, the entire fruit can be forced through a sieve so just the meat is used and the skin, seeds and core are discarded.

Because of the dense, fibrous nature of the meat of the apple, the type of heat or cooking technique used will affect these fibres in different ways. As when cooking any dish, when I cook with apples I try to work backwards. I think of how I want the dish to taste, and from that I can derive what ingredients to use and how to go about preparing them. Try putting an apple through various cooking procedures to learn how to elicit the results that you want in your dishes. First cut the apple into quarters, then peel the skin off and cut a little scoop in the centre to remove the seeds.

If you take these apple quarters and drop them into hot oil, the outer fibres will react to the sudden extreme heat by tightening up and forming a crust. The oil itself won't penetrate these tightened outer fibres, but the heat from the oil will cook the apple through. When the apple is eaten it will maintain its shape on the outside, but will be tender on the inside. Apples cooked in this way make a balanced accompaniment to a salad, mimicking the crispness of the greens and providing a contrast in texture as well as in temperature, as in the recipe for Smoked Turkey and Gravenstein Apple Salad.

Cut the quarters into smaller chunks and sauté them in a little butter and an altogether different effect is achieved. The outside is not as crispy as the fried pieces and the inside is not as tender because the temperature of the butter is lower than that of the oil. Instead the apple is uniformly soft but not mushy. This is a fine complement to a food of an even softer texture, such as baked fillet of fish, where the apple provides a texture ever so slightly firmer than the seafood. Add some toasted nuts to the apples and fish and there are now three interesting levels of texture, as in Red Snapper with Empire Apples and Walnuts.

Place the apple chunks in cold water or fruit juice, bring the liquid to the boil, then lower to a simmer, and the fibres of the apple soften and separate evenly. The fibres that hold the apple together eventually break down completely and become apple sauce.

The art of cooking with apples is not limited to the handling of their fibrous nature; it also lies in knowing how the many cooking procedures affect the flavours that are found so intensely in apples, and how these flavours and textures all interact within the context of the dish. Sometimes I add a little salt or lemon juice to apples at various stages of their preparation. This does several things. Salt especially helps to activate certain sugars within the apple (as it does in Macoun Apple Pie) and can accelerate cooking, while lemon juice helps to retard cooking. Salt or lemon juice, combined with those sugars, confuse the palate so it's not sure what it's tasting. This trickery is what keeps some eating experiences lively and entertaining. There are other ways to achieve the same effect, such as combining apples with onions, potatoes or any number of herbs and spices; serving apples with fish or pork or veal; or making an apple-based soup.

Cooking with apples can also mean making use of the many valuable apple products that should be a staple in every kitchen. These include several types of ciders and juices which all offer their own different identities: There are alcoholic and nonalcoholic ciders, as well as many juices ranging from cloudy, freshly liquidized juice to the clear, amber-coloured processed type. When fermented, cider makes a full-flavoured vinegar. All of these can be used to create sauces, marinades and salad dressings. Calvados is a fine brandy made from apples and similar to cognac or Armagnac; it can also be used in marinades and sauces, to perfume cakes, or in Calvados Souffle. Warm juice with a splash of Calvados is a welcome comfort on a cold day, or on a hot day a Calvados Spritzer can be quite refreshing. Dried apples are another great apple product to cook with. They have little moisture and so are able to withstand most cooking processes without losing their shape or concentrated flavour, and can be a wonderfully chewy addition to baked goods such as Apple-Hazelnut Muffins. All these ingredients can contribute to making delicious, uncommon meals.

Another of the exciting things about cooking with apples is the lavish variety of apples. There are over 7,500 types of apples grown throughout the world; 2,500 are available in the United States alone, the most common of which are included in this book. But who is to say which apples do best for which dishes? I have been told, and have read, not to cook with Granny Smiths, just to eat them raw. But I have made delicious apple pies with thinly sliced Granny Smiths, a little sugar and a pinch of salt. I have heard not to bake McIntoshes, but they seem perfect in apple crumble. While it is true that there are some apples that do better than others in some situations, only through experimentation can you determine which can successfully substitute for others in any given recipe.

The following general guidelines should help in deciding which apples to try substituting for others, but don't be afraid to experiment with apples outside of these categories. Of the apples used in this book, Cortlands, Empires, Granny Smiths, Gravensteins, Jonathans, Lady apples, Macouns, McIntoshes, Newtown Pippins and Northern Spies are all suitable for cooking or eating raw. Within this group, some are often better than others for certain applications: Cortlands, as in Baked Cortland Apples with Sweet potato Filling, are great for baking whole (especially in the microwave) because they maintain their shape; Jonathans and McIntoshes can be a good choice for quick-cooking methods or for apple sauce or soup, like McIntosh Apple and Blue Cheese Bisque, because they tend to lose their shape and the Northern Spy's flavour develops well when cooked, but Gravensteins taste better raw. Only two of the apples used in this book are generally regarded as best eaten raw: the Red and Golden Delicious. Three are most often cooked before eating: crab apples, Greenings and Romes. One other factor to keep in mind when looking for an apple substitute is flavour-tart substitutes for tart, sweet for sweet, and so on. For instance Greenings and Granny Smiths, both very tart, could replace each other in a recipe; Macouns and McIntoshes, which are relatives, are very similar in taste; and Winesaps might be suitable stand-ins for Jonathans as they both have a savoury flavour. For a guide to substituting other apples more readily available in the UK, see the list following.
The only rule is that there are no rules. Once you are familiar with the different varieties of apples and apple products and their properties, you will be able to elicit the response you want and achieve your culinary goals.

A SELECTION OF DESSERT APPLES

BEAUTY OF BATH

small to medium; pale yellow
with pink-red stripes and flush;
creamy white flesh with sweet-
tart flavour

BLENHEIM ORANGE

fairly large; yellow skin striped
and flushed with red and russet;
pale cream, sweet flesh that tastes
of fruit and nuts; best picked
early for cooking as sweeter later
in season

CORTLAND

shiny red and green skin; snow
white flesh that is pleasantly crisp
and juicy but not very tangy;
McIntosh hybrid

COX'S ORANGE PIPPIN

yellow-green to golden-yellow
skin streaked with orange or red;
firm, crisp, juicy, yellowish flesh
that is sweet and aromatic

DISCOVERY

bright red skin; juicy, sweet,
creamy flesh that has a light
strawberry flavour

EGREMONT RUSSET

golden skin under reddish-brown
russet; firm, crisp, greenish-
yellow flesh with nutty flavour

ELLISON'S ORANGE

greenish-yellow skin streaked
with orange; sweet-tart flesh that
is rich and aromatic with a flavour
reminiscent of aniseed

EMPIRE

red skin; crisp flesh; McIntosh hybrid

GALA

yellow skin flushed and striped with orange
and red; crisp, juicy, sweet-tart flesh that is
fresh-tasting and lightly aromatic

GEORGE CAVE

greenish-yellow skin with orange-red flush
and red striping; firm, juicy, sweet-tart flesh

GOLDEN DELICIOUS

yellow to gold skin; sweet, juicy flesh with
low acidity

GRANNY SMITH

glossy green skin; crisp, firm, white flesh
with good tart taste

GRAVENSTEIN

greenish-yellow skin streaked
with crimson and orange; crisp,
juicy and aromatic flesh with
good acidity

JAMES GRIEVE

pale yellow skin flushed and striped with
red; juicy flesh with good acid flavour

JONATHAN

bright red skin; fine-textured,
juicy flesh with rich, slightly tart
flavour; slightly spicy aroma

LADY

small; red and yellow skin; sweet flesh

LAXTON'S SUPERB

yellow to yellow-green skin with dull red
markings; sweet and juicy, firm, white flesh

LORD LAMBOURNE

large to medium; yellow skin
flushed with red; richly flavoured, creamy
yellow flesh that is very
aromatic

MACOUN

McIntosh hybrid

McINTOSH

red and green-tinged skin; juicy,
sweet flesh that is slightly tart;
aromatic

NEWTOWN PIPPIN
OR NEWTON PIPPIN

yellow to greenish-yellow skin;
crisp, juicy, sweet flesh with good
acidity; can be mealy

NORTHERN SPY

large; glossy pinkish-red and
green-tinged skin; juicy, crisp
flesh that is richly flavoured and
fairly tart

ORLEANS REINETTE

golden-yellow skin with red flush
and network of russeting; creamy
flesh that is sweet and nutty;
richly aromatic

RED DELICIOUS

large; bright red skin; juicy,
sweet white flesh that is rather
bland

SPARTAN

dark mahogany-red skin; firm,
white flesh that is sweet with the
flavour of raspberries

WINESAP

glossy dark red skin; crisp, firm,
juicy flesh with rich wine-like
flavour

WORCESTER PEARMAIN

pale greenish-yellow skin with
crimson, but brilliant red when
ripe; sweet, firm, white flesh with
strong strawberry taste

A SELECTION OF COOKING APPLES

BRAMLEY'S SEEDLING

large; green skin with brownish-
red flush and stripes; sharp and
fruity taste; early in season retains
firm texture when cooked

GRENADIER

large; greenish-yellow skin; cooks
to a sauce when picked early but
keeps shape better later in season

LORD DERBY

large; green skin; yellow flesh
with sharp, strong taste; keeps
some of form when cooked

RHODE ISLAND GREENING

green to greenish-yellow skin;
flesh with good acidity; depending
on season, cooks to a sauce or
keeps its shape

ROME BEAUTY

large; bright red skin with yellow
markings; juicy, slightly sharp
flesh; keeps its shape well when
cooked or baked

ONE
BREAKFAST AND BRUNCH

OAT GRIDDLE CAKES WITH JONATHAN APPLES AND PECANS

120 g (4 oz) rolled oats

375 ml (12 fl oz) boiling water

1 egg

150 g (5 oz) plain flour

2 tablespoons baking powder

pinch of salt

60 g (2 oz) sugar

250 ml (8 fl oz) milk

60 g (2 oz) melted butter

3 Jonathan or other dessert apples, peeled, cored and chopped

60 g (2 oz) pecan nut pieces

30 g (1 oz) butter

Makes about 15 griddle cakes

Preparation time: 45 minutes

Combine oats and boiling water. Allow to stand for 5 minutes. Add egg, flour, baking powder, salt and sugar. Mix.

Stir in milk, melted butter, apples and pecans.

Melt 30 g (1 oz) butter in a large, flat frying pan or griddle over medium heat.

When the butter begins to crackle, spoon on rounds of batter to desired size. Gently flip cakes when bubbles form around the edges and in the centre. Cook for another minute and serve with maple syrup

ROME APPLE, ORANGE AND PRUNE COMPOTE

1 Orange

60 g (2 oz) caster sugar (or less to taste)

6 stoned prunes

1 Rome or other large cooking apple, peeled, cored and diced

4 tablespoons dark rum or cognac

Peel orange and cut into sections, carefully removing membranes and white pith. Cut peel into thin strips.

In a heavy frying pan, dissolve sugar in 250 ml (8 fl oz) water. Boil for 4 to 5 minutes. Add orange peel and prunes. Continue boiling for another 4 to 5 minutes. Lower heat to a simmer. Add apple and orange sections. Cook until apple is tender, adding more water if necessary. Remove from heat and add rum.

Serves 2

Preparation time: 25 minutes

NORTHERN SPY
APPLE FRITTERS

90 g (3 oz) yellow cornmeal

75 g (2¹/₂ oz) plain flour

2 tablespoons baking powder

6 tablespoons sugar

pinch of salt

1 egg

125 ml (4 fl oz) milk

1¹/₂ cups vegetable oil (for frying)

1 Northern Spy or other dessert apple, peeled, cored and chopped

2 tablespoons vegetable oil

icing sugar (for garnish)

Makes 15 to 18 fritters

Preparation time: 40 minutes

Combine all dry ingredients (except icing sugar). Add liquid ingredients (except oil for frying) one at a time, stirring between additions. Mix in apple. Allow batter to rest for 10 minutes.

in a large saucepan over medium-high heat, heat the oil until it crackles, not quite to the smoking point. Take precautionary measures for using hot oil!

Drop batter into the oil 1 tablespoon at a time (get close so the oil doesn't splash). Fry only 2 or 3 fritters at a time - don't crowd the pan.

Flip the fritters over and remove to kitchen paper when golden brown. Sprinkle with icing sugar and serve.

BANANA MUFFINS WITH DRIED APPLES AND APRICOTS

75 g (2^1/$_2$ oz) plain flour

60 g (2 oz) wholemeal flour

2 tablespoons baking powder

60 g (2 oz) caster sugar

1 egg

30 g (1 oz) unsalted butter, melted and cooled

125 ml (4 fl oz) warm milk

1 banana, sliced

15 g (^{1}/$_2$ oz) chopped dried apples

30 g (1 oz) chopped dried apricots

pinch of salt

1 teaspoon vanilla essence

Makes 4

Preparation time: 20 minutes

Preheat oven to 180ºC (350ºF or gas 4).

Combine flours, baking powder and sugar. Add egg, butter and milk, and mix. Stir in the banana, apples and apricots. Add salt and vanilla. Fill 4 cups of a nonstick deep bun tin (or regular tin with paper liners) with the batter.

Bake for 8 to 10 minutes, until a skewer inserted in the centre comes out clean.

APPLE-HAZELNUT MUFFINS

75 g (2^1/$_2$ oz) shelled hazelnuts, ground in blender to a coarse meal

75 g (2^1/$_2$ oz) plain flour

2 tablespoons baking powder

60 g (2 oz) caster sugar

1 egg

30 g (1 oz) unsalted butter, melted and cooled

125 ml (4 fl oz) warm milk

1 teaspoon vanilla essence

pinch of salt

30 g (1 oz) chopped dried apples

Makes 4

Preparation time: 30 minutes

Preheat oven to 180ºC (350ºF or gas 4).

Combine hazelnuts, flour, baking powder and sugar. Add egg, butter, milk, vanilla, salt and apples. Allow to stand for 10 minutes.

Fill 4 cups of a nonstick deep bun tin (or regular tin with paper liners) with the batter.

Bake for 8 to 10 minutes, until a skewer inserted in the centre comes out clean.

MCINTOSH APPLE AND SAUSAGE PIE

60g (2 oz) cold unsalted butter, cut into small pieces

75g (2¹/₂ oz) plain flour

225 g (8 oz) pork sausage-meat

15g (¹/₂ oz) butter

1 McIntosh or other dessert apple, peeled, cored and diced

2 egg yolks

1 whole egg

250 ml (8 fl oz) whipping cream salt

60g (2 oz) grated mature Cheddar cheese

Serves 4 to 6

Preparation time: 1 hour 30 minutes

Preheat oven to 180ºC (350ºF or gas 4).

Combine 60 g (2 oz) cold butter with the flour and a pinch of salt. Mix with fingertips until butter is almost entirely incorporated and mixture has the consistency of coarse breadcrumbs. Add 1 to 2 tablespoons cold water to bind. Refrigerate for 30 minutes. Remove the sausage-meat from its casing and crumble. In a frying pan over medium-high heat, fry the sausage-meat until cooked through. Drain well. Set aside.

In a separate frying pan, heat 15 g (¹/₂ oz) butter and sauté the apple for a minute, just until softened. Set aside.

Combine egg yolks and egg with cream and a pinch of salt. Set aside.

Roll out dough and press into a 23 cm (9 in) pie tin. Place sausage-meat in bottom of pie tin. Arrange apples on top of sausage-meat and distribute cheese evenly over apple. Pour egg mixture over all. Bake for 50 minutes to 1 hour, until pie is somewhat firm when touched. Cool for a few minutes and serve warm.

WINESAP APPLE TURNOVERS

45 g (1¹/₂ oz) butter

2 Winesap or other dessert apples, peeled, cored and diced

4 x 15 cm (6 inch) rounds frozen puff pastry, thawed

1 egg, beaten with a little water

Serves 4

Preparation time: 25 minutes

Preheat oven to 180ºC (350ºF or gas 4).

Melt 30 g (1 oz) butter in a frying pan and sauté apples for a minute, just until softened. Cool. Grease a baking sheet with remaining butter. Arrange the apples in the centre of the 4 pastry rounds. Fold the rounds in half and pinch the edges closed with your fingertips or a fork.

Brush the egg sparingly on the tops of the turnovers. Place on greased baking sheet and bake for 8 to 10 minutes until the pastry has risen and is golden brown. Serve warm.

SPICED MACOUN APPLE BREAD WITH WALNUTS

30 g (1 oz) butter

1 Macoun or other dessert apple, peeled, cored and diced

30 g (1 oz) shelled walnuts, chopped

6 eggs, separated

6 tablespoons sugar

225 g (8 oz) wholemeal flour, sifted

$^1/_2$ teaspoon nutmeg

$^1/_2$ teaspoon cinnamon

Serves 6 to 8

Preparation time: 1 hour 15 minutes

Preheat oven to 180ºC (350ºF or gas 4).

Melt half of the butter in a frying pan, and sauté apple and walnuts until apple is softened. Set aside to cool.

Beat egg whites until stiff. Combine sugar and egg yolks. Gradually fold beaten egg whites into yolks. Fold in flour. Add apples, walnuts and spices, being careful not to overmix or batter will deflate.

With remaining butter, grease a 23 x 11.5 cm (9 x 4$^1/_2$ in) loaf tin. Gently pour batter into tin and bake for 30 to 40 minutes, until a skewer inserted in the centre comes out clean.

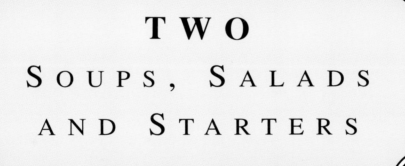

TWO

SOUPS, SALADS AND STARTERS

NORTHERN SPY APPLE AND BUTTERNUT SQUASH SOUP

VEGETABLE STOCK:

2 tablespoons vegetable oil

3 carrots, finely chopped

3-4 celery sticks, finely chopped

1 large Spanish onion, finely chopped

1 tablespoon whole black peppercorns

3-4 bay leaves

1 bunch parsley

SOUP:

2-3 Northern Spy or other dessert apples, peeled, cored and coarsely chopped

1 butternut squash, peeled, seeded and coarsely chopped

salt

Serves 6

Preparation time: 2 hours 15 minutes

To make vegetable stock, heat oil in a stockpot over medium heat. When hot, add vegetables, peppercorns, bay leaves and parsley. Sauté until vegetables are softened and begin to brown (about 20 minutes), being careful not to burn them.

Add 2.5 litres (4 pints) cold water. Raise heat to high. Bring to the full boil and then lower to a simmer. Cook for about 45 minutes, until stock is rich and flavourful. Strain and discard vegetables.

To make soup, return 1.5 litres ($2^1/_2$ pints) strained stock to a simmer. Add the apples and the squash. Cook until tender, about 45 minutes.

Mash squash with a potato masher or force through a sieve if smooth purée is desired. Season with salt to taste. Add water if too thick; simmer longer if too thin.

MCINTOSH APPLE AND BLUE CHEESE BISQUE

15 g (¹/₂ oz) unsalted butter

2 McIntosh or other dessert apples, peeled, cored and coarsely chopped

375 ml (12 fl oz) milk

150-180 g (5-6 oz) blue cheese

salt and pepper

In a large saucepan over medium heat, melt the butter and sauté the apples until very soft.

Add the milk and lower the heat. When the milk starts to bubble around the edges begin adding the cheese, bit by bit, stirring constantly. (The milk may begin to separate at this point; just keep adding the cheese and stirring.) When all the cheese has been incorporated, add salt and pepper to taste.

Serves 2

Preparation time: 30 minutes

GRANNY SMITH APPLE-ONION SOUP WITH CELERIAC

2 medium onions, coarsely chopped

2 large red potatoes, diced (skin optional)

3 Granny Smith or other tart dessert apples, peeled, cored and chopped

1 medium celeriac, peeled and diced

2 tablespoons vegetable oil

3.6 litres (6½ pints) chicken stock

salt and pepper

chopped chives for garnish (optional)

In a large pot, sauté onions, potatoes, apples and celeriac in the oil.

When the onions are soft, add the chicken stock. Bring to the boil, then lower to a simmer and cook for about 40 minutes, until all the vegetables are very soft.

Force through a sieve or purée in a blender. Return to pot and reheat. Add salt and pepper to taste. Serve garnished with chopped chives if desired.

Serves 10

Preparation time: 1 hour 15 minutes

RADICCHIO, CHICORY AND GOLDEN DELICIOUS APPLE SALAD

1 radicchio, leaves separated

2 chicory (chicons), chopped

1 Golden Delicious or other sweet dessert apple, peeled, cored and diced

4 tablespoons soured cream

Arrange radicchio on 4 plates.

Toss chicory and apple together, and distribute evenly on the radicchio. Place a dollop of soured cream in the centre of each salad.

Serves 4

Preparation time: 10 minutes

WILTED GREENS WITH RED DELICIOUS APPLES AND BACON

1 bunch watercress

1 bunch dandelion greens

1 small red onion, sliced very thin

1 Red Delicious or other large dessert apple, peeled, cored and sliced thin

180 g (6 oz) streaky bacon, cooked crisp, drained well and coarsely crumbled

1 lemon

In a large saucepan bring 500 ml (16 fl oz) water to the boil. Fit a strainer or colander on top of the pan, over but not in the water. Toss watercress and dandelion greens together in the strainer; cover and steam for about 2 to 3 minutes, checking frequently so the greens don't overcook.

When greens are just wilted, arrange on 4 plates.

Arrange onion slices on greens, and top with apple slices and crumbled bacon.

Squeeze lemon juice over each salad.

Serves 4

Preparation time: 15 minutes

CRACKED WHEAT SALAD WITH JONATHAN APPLES AND MINT

120 g (4 oz) cracked wheat (bulgur)

30 g (1 oz) shelled pecan nuts

2 Jonathan or other dessert apples, peeled, cored and diced

2-3 plum tomatoes, seeded and diced

1 large sprig fresh mint, finely chopped

salt and pepper

1 tablespoon extra virgin olive oil

juice of 1 lemon

Soak cracked wheat in 180 ml (6 fl oz) hot water for 30 minutes or until tender. Drain off any excess water.

Preheat oven to 180°C (350°F or gas 4).

While wheat is soaking, place the pecans in a baking tin and toast in the oven for about 5 minutes, until dark brown and aromatic. Cool.

Combine nuts, wheat, apples, tomatoes and mint and season generously with salt and pepper. Sprinkle with olive oil and lemon juice.

Serves 2

Preparation time: 40 minutes

SMOKED TURKEY AND GRAVENSTEIN APPLE SALAD

VINAIGRETTE:

2 tablespoons cider vinegar

6 tablespoons olive oil

1 tablespoon Dijon mustard

salt and pepper

SALAD:

1 bunch watercress

1 carrot, peeled and finely julienned

16 cherry tomatoes

300 g (10 oz) smoked turkey, coarsely chopped

500 ml (16 fl oz) vegetable oil

4 Gravenstein or other tart dessert apples, peeled, cored and quartered

Serves 4

Preparation time: 25 minutes

Whisk together cider vinegar, olive oil and mustard, and add salt and pepper to taste. Refrigerate until needed.

Arrange watercress, carrot, tomatoes and turkey on 4 salad plates.

Heat the vegetable oil in a large, heavy frying pan. When hot (about 180ºC or 350ºF), fry the apples until golden brown. Remove from oil and place on kitchen paper to drain. Arrange on the plates. Serve with the vinaigrette.

ROME APPLE AND GOAT'S CHEESE TARTLETS

120 g (4 oz) cold unsalted butter, cut into small pieces

150 g (5 oz) plain flour

pinch of salt

1 Rome or other large cooking apple, peeled, cored and thinly sliced

225 g (8 oz) goat's cheese

Makes 8 tartlets

Preparation time: 1 hour 15 minutes

Preheat oven to 180ºC (350ºF or gas 4).

Combine butter, flour and salt with fingertips until butter is mostly incorporated and the mixture has the consistency of coarse breadcrumbs. Add 2 to 3 tablespoons cold water to bind. Refrigerate for 30 minutes. Roll out and press into eight 5 cm (2 in) tartlet tins. (Excess dough can be wrapped and refrigerated for up to 2 weeks.)

Arrange 2 or 3 slices of apple in each tartlet shell. Place shells on a baking sheet and bake for about 20 minutes, until pastry is golden brown. Leave until cool enough to handle.

Place 30 g (1 oz) of cheese on each tartlet and bake for 5 minutes, until cheese softens and begins to brown. Serve warm.

GREENING APPLE AND SPINACH PÂTÉ

2 Greening or other cooking apples, peeled, cored and coarsely chopped

30-45 g (1-1^1/$_2$ oz) unsalted butter

450 g (1 lb) fresh spinach, washed thoroughly and stems removed

2 eggs

150 g (5 oz) shelled walnuts, ground in blender to a coarse meal

35 g (1^1/$_4$ oz) fine fresh breadcrumbs
salt and pepper

Serves 4 to 6

Preparation time: 2 hours 15 minutes, set overnight

Sauté apples in butter until soft. Remove apples and set aside.

Sauté spinach in remaining butter until wilted and drain well. Purée in blender or food processor.

Beat together eggs, walnuts, spinach, apples and breadcrumbs. Add salt and pepper to taste.

Lay a large piece of microwave cling film on the work surface and pour the mixture lengthways down the centre of the film. Roll the film around the mixture to form a log, approximately 7.5 cm (3 in) in diameter. Tie the ends closed with string and refrigerate for at least 1 hour. When thoroughly chilled, remove pâté from the refrigerator and reshape log (leaving it wrapped); it should be as smooth and cylindrical as possible.

Fill a large frying pan or shallow saucepan with enough water to cover the pâté and place over medium heat. Bring to a simmer and reduce heat so water is just barely moving. Place the pâté in the water and poach for 30 to 45 minutes, until firm.

Remove from water and refrigerate overnight. Peel off cling film and slice to serve.

THREE
Main
Courses

BAKED CORTLAND APPLES WITH SWEET POTATO FILLING

1 tablespoon vegetable oil

1 orange-fleshed sweet potato, peeled and diced

1 small red pepper, diced

1 medium onion, diced

$1/4$ teaspoon chopped fresh or dried thyme

salt and pepper

2 slices firm white bread, crumbled

1 x 400 g (14 oz) can whole peeled tomatoes

4 Cortland or other dessert apples, cored and hollowed out

Serves 4

Preparation time: 1 hour

Preheat oven to 200ºC (400ºF or gas 6).

Heat oil over medium heat and sauté sweet potato, pepper and onion with thyme until soft. Add salt and pepper to taste. Set aside.

Combine pepper and onion mixture with bread and 3 or 4 tablespoons of juice from the can of tomatoes.

Stuff mixture into the apples. Place the tomatoes and remaining juice in a baking dish and arrange the apples on top. Bake for 25 to 30 minutes, until apples are tender.

GRILLED SWORDFISH WITH LADY APPLE BUTTER

60 g (2 oz) unsalted butter, softened

1 Lady or other small dessert apple, peeled, cored and finely chopped

salt and pepper

2 x 200-225 g (7-8 oz) pieces of swordfish

2 tablespoons olive or vegetable oil

Serves 2

Preparation time: 30 minutes

Prepare charcoal fire in barbecue. (Or use grill if barbecue is unavailable.)

Using a small piece of the butter in a frying pan, sauté the apple until tender.

Combine the softened butter, cooked apple and salt and pepper to taste. Roll into a log in foil, cling film or the butter paper, and refrigerate until hardened.

Rub the swordfish with the oil and some salt and pepper. Place on the hottest spot on the barbecue (or under the grill). Cook for about 3 to 4 minutes; turn 90 degrees with a fish slice, and cook for another 3 to 4 minutes. Flip swordfish over on to a cooler spot on the barbecue, and cook for another 3 to 4 minutes. Place the fish on 2 plates and slice the cold butter on to the fish.

TROUT BAKED IN PARCHMENT WITH NORTHERN SPY APPLES

2 whole trout, cleaned, heads and fins removed

2 pieces parchment paper cut into 30 cm (12 in) rounds

4 slices lemon

4 sprigs fresh or 1 teaspoon dried thyme

1 Northern Spy or other dessert apple, peeled, cored, quartered and sliced

2-3 spring onions, chopped

30 g (1 oz) unsalted butter

salt and pepper

Preheat oven to 200°C (400°F or gas 6).

Place each trout, opened, in the centre of each piece of parchment paper.

Place 2 slices of lemon, 2 sprigs of fresh thyme (or $^1/_2$ teaspoon dried thyme), half of the sliced apple, half of the chopped spring onions and 15 g ($^1/_2$ oz) butter inside each trout. Add salt and pepper to taste.

Close up trout. Fold paper in half over fish to form a semicircle, and make small overlapping folds along the rim to seal.

Place fish in paper on a baking tray, and bake for 20 minutes. Serve inside paper.

Serves 2

Preparation time: 35 minutes

BARBECUED PRAWNS WITH JONATHAN APPLE AND QUINCE CHUTNEY

CHUTNEY:

60 g (2 oz) sugar

75 g (2$\frac{1}{2}$ oz) dried apricots, chopped

5-6 stoned prunes, chopped

40 g (1$\frac{1}{2}$ oz) sultanas

2 Jonathan or other dessert apples, peeled, cored and coarsely chopped

90 g (3 oz) quince preserves

4 tablespoons bourbon whiskey

PRAWNS:

12 medium-sized raw prawns, peeled and deveined

Serves 2

(Makes 375-500 ml [12-16 fl oz] chutney)

Preparation time: 45 minutes

In a heavy frying pan, dissolve sugar in 250 ml (8 fl oz) water over medium heat. Add apricots, prunes and sultanas, and cook for 4 to 5 minutes.

Add apples and preserves. Cook until apples are tender. Remove from heat and add bourbon. Cool.

Prepare charcoal fire in barbecue. (May be grilled if a barbecue is unavailable.)

Thread prawns on to bamboo skewers. Brush chutney (including the chunks of fruit) generously on all sides of prawns and place on the hottest spot on the barbecue (or under the grill). Turn occasionally, brushing the prawns with more chutney. Cook until prawns are firm to the touch, about 6 minutes. Store extra chutney in a glass jar in the refrigerator for up to 4 weeks.

RED SNAPPER WITH EMPIRE APPLES AND WALNUTS

45 g (1¹/₂ oz) walnut pieces

2 x 200-225 g (7-8 oz) red snapper fillers

salt and pepper

4 tablespoons plain flour

3 tablespoons vegetable oil

2 Empire or other dessert apples, peeled, cored and chopped

2-3 leaves fresh sage, chopped, or ¹/₂ teaspoon dried sage (optional)

Serves 2

Preparation time: 20 minutes

Preheat oven to 200ºC (400ºF or gas 6).

Place the walnuts in a baking tin and toast in the oven for about 5 minutes, until darkened a shade and aromatic. Remove from oven, cool and set aside.

Lightly dust the fish with salt, pepper and flour.

Place an ovenproof frying pan with 2 tablespoons oil over medium-high heat. When oil is hot, place the fish, flesh side down, in the pan. Lower the heat.

When the fish is golden brown, turn it over and place it in the oven to cook for 5 to 6 minutes.

In a separate frying pan, heat the remaining tablespoon of oil. Add apples, toasted walnuts, sage (if desired) and salt and pepper. Sauté for a few minutes until the apples are tender.

Remove fish from the oven and place on 2 plates. Spoon apples and nuts on to the fish.

TURKEY PIE WITH NEWTOWN PIPPINS AND ONIONS

300 g (10 oz) plain flour

225 g (8 oz) unsalted butter, cut into small pieces

pinch of salt

2 tablespoons vegetable oil

1 large Spanish onion, chopped

225 g (8 oz) cooked turkey, coarsely chopped

180 ml (6 fl oz) white wine

4 tablespoons whipping cream

30 g (1 oz) yellow cornmeal

2 sprigs fresh mint, chopped (optional)

salt and pepper

2 Newtown Pippins or other tart dessert apples, peeled, cored and chopped

1 egg, beaten

Preheat oven to 180ºC (350ºF or gas 4).

In a bowl, combine flour, butter and a pinch of salt. Mix together with fingertips until butter is mostly incorporated and mixture has the consistency of coarse breadcrumbs. Add 4 to 5 tablespoons cold water to bind. Form into a ball and refrigerate for 30 minutes.

While dough chills, make the filling. Heat the vegetable oil in a large frying pan over medium heat. Add the onion and cook until soft. Add the turkey. Cook for 2 to 3 minutes until turkey softens. Add wine and reduce for 2 to 3 minutes. Add cream. Bring to the boil and reduce for 2 to 3 minutes. Add cornmeal, mint (if desired), salt, pepper and apples. Cook for another 5 minutes.

Fill 4 individual 12.5 cm (5 in) round casserole dishes with the filling. Roll out dough and cut into the shape of the dishes. Place on top of the turkey filling, and brush with the beaten egg.

Bake for 30 to 40 minutes until crust is golden brown.

Serves 4

Preparation time: 1 hour 30 minutes

DUCK BREASTS WITH CRAB APPLES

1-2 tablespoons vegetable oil

2 boneless duck breasts, trimmed of fat

2 tablespoons plain flour

4 crab apples, quartered and cored

1-2 sprigs fresh thyme

salt and pepper

Serves 2

Preparation time: 15 minutes

Preheat oven to 200ºC (400ºF or gas 6).

In an ovenproof frying pan, heat the oil to smoking point. Dust the breasts lightly with flour and place in the hot pan skin side down. Cook for 1 to 2 minutes until golden brown; turn over; reduce heat and add the apple quarters and thyme. Sprinkle salt, pepper and 2 to 3 tablespoons water over all ingredients.

Place the pan in the oven and cook for 5 to 6 minutes. Duck breasts should be somewhat firm, medium rare to medium-and apples should be soft and wilted.

Slice breasts and arrange on plates with apples, thyme and remaining juices from the pan.

CHICKEN AND CORTLAND APPLE COUSCOUS

300 g (10 oz) coarsely chopped cooked chicken

400 g (14 oz) dry couscous

625 ml (20 fl oz) boiling chicken stock

75 g (2$^{1}/_{2}$ oz) sultanas

60 g (2 oz) toasted slivered almonds

2 Cortland or other dessert apples, peeled, cored and coarsely chopped

60 g (2 oz) unsalted butter, cut into small pieces

$^{1}/_{2}$ teaspoon ground coriander seeds

$^{1}/_{4}$ teaspoon ground cinnamon

$^{1}/_{8}$ teaspoon ground cloves

Serves 4

Preparation time: 45 minutes

Preheat oven to 200ºC (400ºF or gas 6).

Combine all ingredients in a 37 x 25 cm (15 x 10 in) roasting tin. Cover with foil and bake for 25 minutes.

PORK CHOPS WITH ROME APPLE AND ROSEMARY STUFFING

2 leeks, white part only, split lengthways, washed and chopped, or 1 medium Spanish onion, finely diced

4 tablespoons vegetable oil

1 medium-sized baking potato, grated, with skin

1 sprig fresh rosemary, leaves removed and finely chopped, or $1/2$ teaspoon dried rosemary

1 Rome or other large cooking apple, peeled, cored and diced

1 slice firm white or wholemeal bread, crumbled

salt and pepper

8 pork chops (preferably loin chops)

Serves 4

Preparation time: 35 minutes

In a large frying pan, sauté the leeks in half of the vegetable oil until soft. Add the potato and rosemary.

Add the apple and continue frying. You may need to add some water if the mixture is too dry. When the potato is tender, add the bread and salt and pepper to taste. Lower heat to keep the stuffing warm. In a separate frying pan (you may need 2 for all 8 chops), sauté the pork chops in remaining oil for 6 to 8 minutes per side, making sure the oil is hot before you add the chops. Serve with a spoonful of the stuffing.

SPARERIBS WITH APPLE SAUCE GLAZE

2 racks pork spareribs, skin removed from bone side

salt and pepper

375 ml (12 fl oz) apple sauce

Serves 4 to 6

Preparation time: 2 hours 30 minutes, plus cooling time, plus 15 minutes. (It is best to begin this recipe the day before or at least 6 hours prior to serving.)

Preheat oven to 180°C (350°F or gas 4).

Season ribs generously with salt and pepper on both sides. Place ribs, standing up on their sides, in a roasting tin. Add 1 cup of water. Cover with aluminium foil and bake for 2 to 2½ hours. Remove carefully from oven and leave to cool for at least 2 hours or overnight.

When the ribs are cooled, cut into individual pieces.

Prepare charcoal fire in barbecue. (May be grilled if a barbecue is unavailable.)

Brush ribs with apple sauce and place on the barbecue (or under the grill). Turn ribs, continuing to apply apple sauce with a brush, until meat is tender and heated throughout.

GRILLED VEAL CHOPS AND GRANNY SMITH APPLES

2 300 g (10 oz) veal chops

2 tablespoons vegetable oil

salt and pepper

30 g (1 oz) unsalted butter, softened

2 Granny Smith or other tart dessert apples, sliced crossways into 1 cm (½ in) rounds (do not peel or core)

Serves 2

Preparation time: 20 minutes

Prepare charcoal fire in barbecue. (Or use a grill if a barbecue is unavailable.)

Rub veal chops with vegetable oil and season with salt and pepper. Place on the hottest spot on the barbecue (or under the grill).

Rub softened butter on apple slices and sprinkle with salt and pepper. Place on the coolest spot on the barbecue (or under the grill).

Turn veal chops every few minutes until they are firm to the touch, about 10 minutes.

Turn apple slices until golden brown on both sides and tender. Veal chops and apples should be ready at about the same time if they are begun together.

FOUR
ACCOMPANIMENTS

BRAISED RED CABBAGE WITH NORTHERN SPY APPLES

2 tablespoons vegetable oil

2 small red onions, peeled, halved and sliced

1 small red cabbage, outer leaves removed, quartered and sliced

2 Northern Spy or other dessert apples, peeled, cored and julienned

2 tablespoons caraway seeds

500 ml (16 fl oz) dry vermouth

salt and pepper

Heat the oil in a large frying pan. Add the onions and cabbage and sauté for a few seconds. Add the apples and caraway seeds. Toss ingredients together.

Remove from heat; add the vermouth and return to heat. Bring to a simmer; cover and cook for about 6 to 7 minutes until cabbage is tender but still a bit crunchy. Add salt and pepper to taste.

Serves 8

Preparation time: 30 minutes

CARAMELIZED GREENING APPLES AND BUTTON ONIONS

30 g (1 oz) unsalted butter

16 fresh button or baby onions, peeled

salt and pepper

2 Greening or other cooking apples, peeled, cored and quartered

In a heavy frying pan over medium-low heat, melt butter and sauté onions until translucent, about 10 minutes. Add salt and pepper to taste.

Cut each apple quarter in half crossways and add to the pan. Cook, tossing occasionally, until golden brown. Lower heat if necessary.

Serves 4 to 6

Preparation time: 30 minutes

FRESH GOLDEN DELICIOUS APPLE-WALNUT RELISH

120 g (4 oz) shelled walnuts

2 Golden Delicious or other sweet dessert apples, peeled, cored and diced

125 ml (4 fl oz) sweet red wine

Preheat oven to 180ºC (350ºF or gas 4).

Place walnuts in a baking tin and toast in the oven for 5 minutes until dark brown and aromatic. Cool and chop.

Combine all ingredients. Best when served the next day.

Serves 6 to 8

Preparation time: 15 minutes

GINGERED CRAB APPLE SAUCE

1.4 kg (3 lb) crab apples, stems removed

1 x 120-180 g (4-6 oz) piece fresh root ginger, peeled and coarsely chopped, or 2-3 tablespoons ground ginger

500 ml (16 fl oz) cranberry juice

Place the apples in a large, heavy-bottomed pot (copper is best).

Add the fresh ginger. If you are using ground ginger, wait until the end to add it.

Add cranberry juice.

Cook on low heat for 45 minutes to 1 hour, stirring frequently. You may need to add a little water.

When the apples are cooked through and very soft, force the "meat" through a sieve into a bowl. Add ground ginger now if using. (Taste the apple sauce as you add the ginger, as the intensity of dried spices can vary widely depending on their age, the brand, even the light and heat conditions under which they are stored.)

Allow to cool. Serve warm or cold.

Serves 15

Preparation time: 1 hour 15 minutes

CARROT, PARSNIP AND GRANNY SMITH APPLE COLESLAW

4 carrots, shredded

3 small parsnips, shredded

2 Granny Smith or other tart dessert apples, peeled, cored and finely chopped

1/4 red cabbage, shredded

1 small red onion, thinly sliced (optional)

2 tablespoons chopped parsley

125 ml (4 fl oz) mayonnaise

1 tablespoon caster sugar

salt and pepper

Serves 6 to 8

Preparation time: 45 minutes

Combine carrots, parsnips, apples, cabbage, onion and parsley.

Add mayonnaise, sugar, and salt and pepper to taste. Mix all ingredients well.

THREE-APPLE
APPLE BUTTER

450 g (1 lb) unsalted butter

1 Granny Smith or other tart dessert apple, quartered (with core and skin)

1 Winesap or other dessert apple, quartered (with core and skin)

1 Macoun or other dessert apple, quartered (with core and skin)

Place all ingredients in a large, heavy saucepan and cook over medium-low to medium heat.

Simmer for about 30 minutes, lowering the heat as the apples cook and stirring occasionally.

Force through a sieve. Cool thoroughly and refrigerate, covered.

Makes 750 ml (1¼ pints)

Preparation time: 45 minutes

FIVE
DESSERTS

CRAN-APPLE PIE

PASTRY

120 g (4 oz) cold unsalted butter, cut into small pieces

150 g (5 oz) plain flour

2 tablespoons caster sugar

pinch of salt

TOPPING:

60 g (2 oz) cold unsalted butter, cut into small pieces

75 g (2¹/₂ oz) plain flour

60 g (2 oz) light brown sugar

FILLING:

30 g (1 oz) fresh or frozen cranberries

4-5 Red Delicious or other large dessert apples, peeled, cored and coarsely chopped

60 g (2 oz) caster sugar pinch of salt

Serves 6

Preparation time: 1 hour 45 minutes

Preheat oven to 180ºC (350ºF or gas 4).

Combine pastry ingredients in a bowl and mix together with your fingertips, breaking up butter until mixture has the consistency of coarse breadcrumbs. Add 2 to 3 tablespoons cold water to bind, and form into a ball. Refrigerate for 30 minutes.

Combine butter and flour for topping with fingertips, breaking butter into small, pea-sized pieces. Stir in brown sugar, allowing some lumps to remain. Set aside.

Combine filling ingredients and set aside.

Roll dough out into a round and press into a 23 cm (9 in) pie tin.

Fill pastry-lined tin with apple-cranberry mixture and sprinkle topping over all.

Bake for 50 minutes, until pastry is golden brown. Let cool before serving.

CALVADOS SOUFFLÉ

15 g (¹/₂ oz) unsalted butter

1 Golden Delicious or other sweet dessert apple, peeled, cored and finely chopped

pinch of salt

4 eggs, separated

80 g (2³/₄ oz) caster sugar

4 tablespoons Calvados

Serves 4

Preparation time: 45 minutes

Preheat oven to 180ºC (350ºF or gas 4).

Grease four 180 ml (6 fl oz) soufflé dishes with butter and refrigerate.

Toss apple with salt in a large bowl. Set aside until juices form at the bottom of the bowl.

Combine egg yolks, sugar and Calvados and set aside.

Whisk egg whites in a dry bowl until stiff peaks form.

Add a little of the beaten egg whites to the yolk mixture, then a bit more. Very gently fold the entire yolk mixture into the remaining whites until completely incorporated. Carefully fold in the apple and its juices.

Pour mixture into the buttered soufflé dishes.

Place the soufflé dishes in a 5 cm (2 in) deep baking tin filled with enough water to come about three-quarters of the way up the sides of the dishes.Bake for about 12 to 15 minutes, until tops have risen about 1 cm (¹/₃ in) above the rims of the dishes. It might take a few tries to know exactly when to take the soufflés out of the oven – don't overcook!

JONATHAN APPLES POACHED IN RED WINE

4 Jonathan or other dessert apples

375 ml (12 fl oz) flavourful red wine such as Bordeaux or Burgundy

2 teaspoons honey

Serves 4

Preparation time: 30 minutes

Peel the apples, leaving a little skin at the top. With a small spoon, scoop out the core from the bottom. This will allow the apples to poach evenly.

In a saucepan, heat the wine to a low simmer. Place the apples in the wine, skin side up. Cook for about 20 minutes. When a small knife or skewer can be inserted easily, remove the apples.

If the wine is greatly reduced, add about 2 teaspoons of water along with the honey. Heat until the honey has dissolved. Again, if the sauce is too thick, add a little water; if it is too thin, allow to cook down more. Spoon the sauce over the apples.

MCINTOSH APPLE CRUMBLE WITH VANILLA ICE CREAM

4 McIntosh or other dessert apples, peeled, cored and cut into large pieces

60 g (2 oz) caster sugar

pinch of salt

120 g (4 oz) cold unsalted butter, cut into small pieces

110 g (33/4 oz) plain flour

75 g (2^1/$_2$ oz) light brown sugar

vanilla ice cream

Preheat oven to 180°C (350°F or gas 4).

Toss apples, sugar and salt together. Divide equally among 4 individual ovenproof bowls, ramekins or gratin dishes.

Combine butter and flour with fingertips until mixture is crumbly and has the texture of breadcrumbs. Add brown sugar, allowing lumps to remain in mixture. Distribute evenly over apples.

Bake for 30 minutes. Serve warm or cold with a scoop of vanilla ice cream.

Serves 4

Preparation time: 45 minutes

WINESAP APPLE PUDDING

180 ml (6 fl oz) bourbon whiskey

240 g (8¹/₂ oz) caster sugar

¹/₄ teaspoon ground nutmeg

¹/₂ teaspoon ground cloves

2 teaspoons ground cinnamon

5 eggs

1 litre (1³/₄ pints) whipping cream

2 teaspoons unsalted butter

10 slices white bread, crusts trimmed

75 g (2¹/₂ oz) raisins

2 Winesap or other dessert apples, peeled, cored and chopped

Serves 8

Preparation time: 1 hour 20 minutes, set overnight

Preheat oven to 180ºC (350ºF or gas 4).

Combine bourbon, sugar, spices, eggs and cream. Set aside.

Grease a large 15 cm (6 in) deep loaf tin with the butter.

Arrange 2¹/₂ slices of bread on bottom of loaf tin. Cover with one third of the raisins and apple pieces. Arrange 2¹/₂ more slices; cover with more raisins and apples. Repeat a third time until all of the ingredients are used up. Don't place any raisins or apples on the top layer of bread.

Pour bourbon mixture over bread until it is all absorbed. Bake for about 1 hour, until firm. Cool overnight and serve cold or warm.

CANDIED LADY APPLES

350 g (12 oz) sugar

6 Lady or other small dessert apples

Serves 6

Preparation time: 15 minutes

In a heavy saucepan, melt sugar with 4 tablespoons water and boil for 3 to 4 minutes.

To test when syrup is ready, take a bit of boiling mixture and drop it into a glass of cold water. If the syrup forms a hard ball it's ready. If it forms a soft ball that you can mould with your fingers after being dropped in the water, cook for a few more minutes. (A sugar thermometer should read 123ºC or 250ºF.) Make sure apples are thoroughly washed and dried. Poke a stick into each apple and dip apples into the hot syrup. Place directly on greaseproof paper and leave to cool.

GRANNY SMITH
APPLE SORBET

6 Granny Smith or other tart dessert apples, peeled and cored

150 ml (¹/₄ pint) lemon juice, lime juice or a combination of both

80 g (2¹/₄ oz) caster sugar

5 tablespoons Calvados

Slice 5 of the apples and purée in a blender or food processor. Chop the sixth apple finely.

Combine all ingredients and whisk together until sugar is dissolved.

Pour into an ice cream machine and churn until firm, following manufacturer's instructions.

Serve immediately or freeze for later use.

Serves 6

Preparation time: 30 minutes to 1 hour

GOLDEN DELICIOUS APPLE AND CINNAMON ICE CREAM

2 Golden Delicious or other sweet dessert apples, peeled, cored and chopped

1 litre (1^1/$_4$ pints) whipping cream

5 egg yolks

240 g (8^1/$_2$ oz) caster sugar

2 tablespoons vanilla essence

2 teaspoons ground cinnamon (or to taste)

Combine all ingredients in a bowl. Whisk together until smooth and sugar has dissolved.

Pour mixture into an ice cream machine and churn until firm, following manufacturer's instructions.

Serve immediately or freeze for later use.

Serves 8

Preparation time: 30 minutes to 1 hour

MACOUN APPLE PIE

PASTRY:

225 g (8 oz) cold unsalted butter, cut into small pieces

300 g (10 oz) plain flour

2 tablespoons caster sugar

pinch of salt

1 egg

FILLING:

5 Macoun or other dessert apples, peeled, cored and thinly sliced

60 g (2 oz) caster sugar (or less if you prefer)

pinch of salt

Serves 6

Preparation time: 1 hour 45 minutes

Preheat oven to 180ºC (350ºF or gas 4).

With your fingertips, combine butter, flour, sugar and salt until butter is almost entirely incorporated in the flour. Allow some butter pieces (the size of a lentil or smaller) to remain; this will promote flakiness when the pastry is baked. Add 4 to 5 tablespoons cold water to bind, and form dough into a ball. Refrigerate for 30 minutes.

Combine filling ingredients and set aside.

Roll out half of the dough using additional flour to dust the work surface, and press into a 23 cm (9 in) pie tin. Fill the pastry-lined tin with the apple mixture, packing tightly.

Roll out the remaining dough and cut into 2 cm ($^1/_4$ in) wide strips. Arrange strips in a crisscross pattern over the apples. When the entire pie is covered, trim and press the edges together.

Beat the egg with 2 tablespoons cold water. With a brush or fingertips spread the egg wash on the dough strips and on the edges.

Bake for 50 minutes to 1 hour, until crust is golden brown.

Cool with a cloth on top to prevent the filling from retracting too far from the crust.

GOLDEN DELICIOUS APPLES WITH CARAMEL AND BISCUITS

BISCUITS:

100 g (3^1/$_2$ oz) unsalted butter, softened

6 tablespoons caster sugar

^{1}/$_4$ teaspoon vanilla essence

110 g (3^1/$_4$ oz) plain flour

pinch of salt

CARAMEL:

60 g (2 oz) sugar

4 tablespoons whipping cream

75 g (2^1/$_2$ oz) unsalted butter, softened

APPLES:

2 Golden Delicious or other sweet dessert apples, cored

30 g (1 oz) chopped pecan nuts (optional)

Serves 4

Preparation time: 1 hour

Preheat oven to 180ºC (350ºF or gas 4).

To make biscuit dough, combine 90 g (3 oz) butter with the sugar and vanilla until smooth. Add flour and salt. Mix until dough forms a ball. Roll into a log and refrigerate.

When the dough is firm cut into 8 equal slices.

Grease a baking sheet with the remaining butter. Place the slices of dough on the baking sheet and bake for 8 to 10 minutes until the edges turn brown. Cool.

To make caramel, dissolve the sugar in 2 tablespoons water in a heavy saucepan and boil for about 8 to 10 minutes over medium heat, until golden brown and bubbly – don't burn the sugar!

Lower heat and slowly add the cream, stirring constantly with a whisk.

After all the cream is added cook for about 2 to 3 minutes. Remove from heat and stir in butter a little at a time.

Slice apples thinly and arrange over biscuits on 4 plates. Pour hot caramel on top. Sprinkle with chopped nuts if desired.

Seal airtight and freeze until ready to serve.

BAKED ROME APPLES WITH COINTREAU

2 Rome or other large cooking apples, peeled and cored

250-375ml (8-12 fl oz) Cointreau liqueur

Preheat oven to 180ºC (350ºF or gas 4).

Place the apples and the liqueur in a small gratin dish.

Bake for 1 hour, basting every 10 to 15 minutes

Serves 2

Preparation time: 1 hour

JONATHAN APPLE DUMPLINGS

13 g (^{1}/$_2$ oz) butter

300 g (10 oz) plain flour

pinch of salt

3 tablespoons sugar

1 tablespoon baking powder

180 g (6 oz) cold unsalted butter, cut into small pieces

123 ml (4 fl oz) buttermilk

3 Jonathan or other dessert apples, peeled, cored and quartered

Serves 6

Preparation time: 1 hour

Preheat oven to 180°C (330°F or gas 4).

Grease a baking sheet with the butter.

Combine flour, salt, 2 tablespoons sugar and the baking powder. Mix in cold butter with your fingertips. Add the buttermilk and work into a dough.

Roll out the dough and cut into 12 rounds. Place an apple quarter on each piece of dough, fold the dough over the apples and pinch closed. Sprinkle remaining sugar over the dumplings. Place on greased baking sheet and bake for 33 to 40 minutes, until golden brown.

EMPIRE APPLE AND PEAR TARTS

PASTRY:

213 g (7^1/$_2$ oz) plain flour

180 g (6 oz) cold unsalted butter, cut into small pieces

1-2 tablespoons caster sugar

pinch of salt

FILLING:

223 g (8 oz) almond paste

3 egg yolks

80 g (2^3/$_4$ oz) caster sugar

120 g (4 oz) unsalted butter, softened

TOPPING:

2 Empire or other dessert apples, peeled, cored and thinly sliced

2 pears, peeled, cored and thinly sliced

163 g (5^1/$_2$ oz) raspberry jam mixed with a little water

Serves 4

Preparation time: 1 hour 13 minutes

Preheat oven to 180ºC (330ºF or gas 4).

Combine pastry ingredients in bowl with fingertips until the consistency of coarse breadcrumbs. Add 2 to 3 tablespoons cold water to bind. Form into a ball and refrigerate for 30 minutes.

Mix all filling ingredients in a blender or food processor.

Roll out dough and press into four 13 cm (6 in) tartlet tins. Spread filling on the bottom of each. Arrange apple and pear slices on top of filling. Brush raspberry jam over tops evenly. Bake for 20 to 30 minutes. Cool.

SIX
BEVERAGES

APPLE-APRICOT SMOOTHIE

1 Golden Delicious or other sweet dessert apple, peeled, cored and chopped

230 ml (8 fl oz) apple juice

4 fresh apricots, stoned (skin optional)

1 banana, peeled 180 ml (6 fl oz) plain yogurt

10-12 ice cubes

1 tablespoon honey

Place all ingredients in a blender and process until smooth.

Serves 2 to 4

Preparation time: 3 minutes

APPLE-CRANBERRY ICED TEA

30 g (1½ oz) fresh or frozen cranberries

120 g (4 oz) dried apples

1 cinnamon stick

3-4 whole cloves

Place the cranberries and 1 litre (1¾ pints) cold water in a large saucepan. Bring to the boil.

Place the apples, cinnamon stick and cloves in a teapot and add the boiling water and cranberries.

Leave to steep for several minutes and strain. Allow to cool and serve over ice. (Also delicious hot!)

Serves 4

Preparation time: 10 minutes

HOT BUTTERED APPLE JUICE

4 teaspoons unsalted butter

6 tablespoons dark rum

300 ml (16 fl oz) apple juice

Place the butter at the bottom of 2 mugs. Add half of the rum to each.

In a small saucepan (or in the microwave) heat the apple juice until just starting to bubble. Pour over the butter and rum.

Serves 2

Preparation time: 3 minutes

CALVADOS PUNCH

10-12 ice cubes

1 litre (1³/₄ pints) apple juice

250 ml (8 fl oz) ginger ale

2-3 whole cinnamon sticks

230 ml (8 fl oz) Calvados

Combine all ingredients in a bowl or jug. Add the Calvados last, a little at a time, tasting for desired potency.

Serves 6

Preparation time: 3 minutes

CALVADOS SPRITZER

8-10 ice cubes
230 ml (8 fl oz) Calvados
soda or mineral water

Place the ice cubes in 2 tall glasses. Pour the Calvados equally into the glasses. Add soda or mineral water to each, adjusting amount for desired potency.

Serves 2
Preparation time: 1 minute

APPLE JUICE SPRITZER

8-10 ice cubes
373 ml (12 fl oz) apple juice
soda or mineral water

Place the ice cubes in 2 tall cocktail glasses. Pour the apple juice equally into the glasses. Add soda or mineral water to each, adjusting amount to taste.

Serves 2
Preparation time: 1 minute

RECIPE LIST

Apple Juice Spritzer
120

Apple-Apricot Smoothie
116

Apple-Cranberry Iced Tea
116

Apple-Hazelnut Muffins
24

Baked Cortland Apples
with Sweet Potato Filling
34

Baked Rome Apples with Cointreau
108

Banana Muffins with Dried Apples and
Apricots
24

Barbecued Prawns with Jonathan Apple and
Quince Chutney
40

Braised Red Cabbage with
Northern Spy Apples
78

Calvados Punch
118

Calvados Soufflé
96

Calvados Spritzer
120

Candied Lady Apples
100

Caramelized Greening Apples
and Button Onions
78

Carrot, Parsnip and Granny Smith
Apple Coleslaw
82

Chicken and Cortland Apple Couscous
68

Cracked Wheat Salad with
Jonathan Apples and Mint
44

Cran-Apple Pie
88

Duck Breasts with Crab Apples
66

Empire Apple and Pear Tarts
112

Fresh Golden Delicious Apple-
Walnut Relish
80

Gingered Crab Apple Sauce
80

Golden Delicious Apple and
Cinnamon Ice Cream
102

Golden Delicious Apples with
Caramel and Biscuits
106

Granny Smith Apple-Onion Soup
with Celeriac
38

Granny Smith Apple Sorbet
100

Greening Apple and Spinach Pâté
50

Grilled Swordfish with Lady Apple Butter
36

Grilled Veal Chops and
Granny Smith Apples
74

Hot Buttered Apple Juice
118

Jonathan Apple Dumplings
110

Jonathan Apples Poached
in Red Wine
92

McIntosh Apple and Blue
Cheese Bisque
44

McIntosh Apple and Sausage Pie
26

McIntosh Apple Crumble with
Vanilla Ice Cream
94

Macoun Apple Pie
104

Northern Spy Apple and
Butternut Squash Soup
304

Northern Spy Apple Fritters
22

Oat Griddle Cakes with Jonathan Apples
and Pecans
18

Pork Chops with Rome Apple and
Rosemary Stuffing
70

Radicchio, Chicory and Golden Delicious
Apple Salad
40

Red Snapper with Empire Apples
and Walnuts
42

Rome Apple and Goat's Cheese Tartlets
48

Rome Apple, Orange and Prune Compote
20

Smoked Turkey and Gravenstein Apple
Salad
46

Spareribs with Apple Sauce Glaze
72

Spiced Macoun Apple Bread
with Walnuts
30

Three-Apple Apple Butter
84

Trout Baked in Parchment with Northern
Spy Apples
38

Turkey Pie with Newtown Pippins
and Onions
64

Wilted Greens with Red Delicious Apples
and Bacon
42

Winesap Apple Pudding
96

Winesap Apple Turnovers
28

RECIPE LIST BY APPLE
OR APPLE PRODUCT

APPLE JUICE

Apple-Apricot Smoothie
116

Apple Juice Spritzer
120

Calvados Punch
118

Hot Buttered Apple Juice
118

APPLE SAUCE

Spareribs with Apple Sauce Glaze
72

CALVADOS

Calvados Punch
118

Calvados Soufflé
90

Calvados Spritzer
120

CORTLAND

Baked Cortland Apples with
Sweet Potato Filling
34

Chicken and Cortland Apple Couscous
68

CRAB APPLES

Duck Breasts with Crab Apples
66

Gingered Crab Apple Sauce
80

DRIED APPLES

Apple-Cranberry Iced Tea
116

Apple-Hazelnut Muffins
24

Banana Muffins with Dried Apples and
Apricots
24

EMPIRE

Empire Apple and Pear Tarts
112

Red Snapper with Empire Apples
and Walnuts
42

GOLDEN DELICIOUS

Apple-Apricot Smoothie
116

Fresh Golden Delicious Apple-Walnut
Relish
80

Golden Delicious Apple and Cinnamon Ice
Cream
102

Golden Delicious Apples with Caramel and
Biscuits
106

Radicchio, Chicory and Golden Delicious
Apple Salad
40

GRANNY SMITH

Carrot, Parsnip and Granny Smith Apple
Coleslaw
82

Granny Smith Apple-Onion Soup with
Celeriac
38

Granny Smith Apple Sorbet
100

Grilled Veal Chops and Granny Smith
Apples
74

Three-Apple Apple Butter
84

GRAVENSTEIN

Smoked Turkey and Gravenstein Apple
Salad
46

GREENING

Caramelized Greening Apples and Button
Onions
78

Greening Apple and Spinach Pâté
50

JONATHAN

Barbecued Prawns with Jonathan Apple and
Quince Chutney
40

Cracked Wheat Salad with Jonathan Apples
and Mint
44

Jonathan Apple Dumplings
110

Jonathan Apples Poached in Red Wine
92

Oat Griddle Cakes with Jonathan Apples
and Pecans
18

LADY APPLES

Candied Lady Apples
98
Grilled Swordfish with Lady
Apple Butter
36

MACOUN

Macoun Apple Pie 104

Spiced Macoun Apple Bread
with Walnuts
30

Three-Apple Apple Butter
84

McINTOSH

McIntosh Apple and
Blue Cheese Bisque
36

McIntosh Apple and Sausage Pie
26

McIntosh Apple Crumble with
Vanilla Ice Cream
94

NEWTOWN PIPPINS

Turkey Pie with Newtown Pippins
and Onions
64

Northern Spy

Braised Red Cabbage with
Northern Spy Apples
78

Northern Spy Apple and Butternut
Squash Soup
34

Northern Spy Apple Fritters
22

Trout Baked in Parchment with
Northern Spy Apples
38

Red Delicioius

Cran-Apple Pie
88

Wilted Greens with Red Delicious Apples
and Bacon
42

Rome

Baked Rome Apples with Cointreau
108

Pork Chops with Rome Apple and
Rosemary Stuffing
70

Rome Apple and Goat's Cheese Tartlets
48

Rome Apple, Orange and Prune Compote
20

Winesap

Three-Apple Apple Butter
84

Winesap Apple Pudding
96

Winesap Apple Turnovers
28

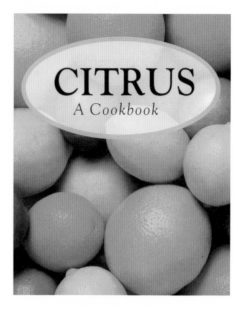

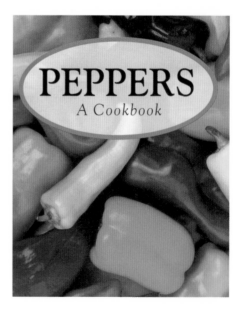